W.B. Yeats and his Circle

Front cover: photograph of W.B. Yeats, c. 1932.
Inside front cover: manuscript draft of Yeats's poem 'The Wild Swans at Coole'
from the collections of the National Library of Ireland.

First published in 1989 by The National Library of Ireland.
© 1989 The National Library of Ireland and the copyright owners of items reproduced.

British Library Cataloguing in Publication Data:
  Fahy, Catherine
    W.B. Yeats and his circle
    I. Poetry in English, Yeats, W.B.
    (William Butler), 1865-1939 —
    Biographies
    I. Title   II. National Library of Ireland
    821'.8
    ISBN 0-907328-15-6

Printed by Mount Salus Press.

Catherine Fahy

W.B. Yeats and his Circle

THE NATIONAL LIBRARY OF IRELAND

1989

Foreword

Since the death of William Butler Yeats on the 28th of January 1939 his family have made three major gifts of his manuscripts to the National Library of Ireland, through Mrs. George Yeats, his widow, in 1958 and 1964, and through Michael Yeats, his son, in 1985.

The collection as a whole constitutes one of the most significant literary archives in the English-speaking world. It includes drafts of Yeats's plays from *The Countess Cathleen* to *Purgatory,* and drafts of the poems published in *Responsibilities, The Wild Swans at Coole, Michael Robartes and the Dancer, The Tower, The Winding Stair, Words for Music Perhaps, A Woman Old and Young* and *Last Poems.* There is also much material relating to *A Vision,* occult notebooks and diaries, juvenilia, letters, corrected proofs and miscellaneous fragments.

On behalf of the National Library and of the Nation I would like to thank the Yeats family for their generosity and public spirit in making these gifts. They have thus ensured that the Yeats manuscripts remain in Ireland. There are many wealthy libraries and private collectors overseas who would have been eager to purchase the Yeats papers, and thus augment the list of literary collections which in the past have been transported abroad.

In order to mark the fiftieth anniversary of the death of William Butler Yeats, the National Library of Ireland has much pleasure in publishing this booklet and in mounting the exhibition of the same title opened by Michael Yeats in the Library on the 30th of January 1989.

I would like to acknowledge the financial assistance of the National Library of Ireland Society and of the National Touring Exhibitions Service of the Department of the Taoiseach in making the publication of this booklet possible.

Anthony G. Hughes
Chairman
Council of Trustees of the National Library of Ireland

William Butler Yeats led an immensely busy and productive life in the course of which he associated, not always amicably, with a great variety of people, some famous in their own right, some remembered today only because of their connection with him. Many of them are mentioned in his writings. This booklet attempts to give faces to some of the names...

1. Yeats and Pollexfen

William Butler Yeats's grandfather was the REVEREND WILLIAM BUTLER YEATS (1), Church of Ireland rector of Tullylish, Co. Down, by all accounts a tolerant and kindly man. His wife, JANE GRACE CORBET (2), was a woman of wit and spirit who wrote poetry which, however, she did not permit anyone to read. Their son JOHN BUTLER YEATS (5), was one of twelve children. While reading law at the Irish Bar he met SUSAN POLLEXFEN (6), the sister of an old school-friend. They married in 1863. WILLIAM POLLEXFEN (3), Susan's father, was of Cornish origin and owned a milling company and shipping firm in Sligo in partnership with the brother of his wife ELIZABETH MIDDLETON (4).

1

1. Rev. William Butler Yeats (1806-62), grandfather.

2. Jane Grace Yeats, née Corbet (1811-76), grandmother.

3. William Pollexfen (1811-92), maternal grandfather.

4. Elizabeth Pollexfen, née Middleton (1819-92), maternal grandmother.

5. John Butler Yeats (1839-1922), father.

6. Susan Yeats, née Pollexfen (1841-1900), mother.

2

3

4

5

6

7

John Butler Yeats and Susan Pollexfen had six children of whom four survived, WILLIAM BUTLER (9), the eldest, born in 1865, SUSAN MARY and ELIZABETH CORBET (8), known as Lily and Lollie respectively, and JOHN (7), known as Jack.

In 1867 John Butler Yeats gave up the practice of law and embarked on a career as an artist, against the wishes of both his own family and the Pollexfens. He moved Susan and the children to London and worked hard at his painting, but as he was neither practical nor businesslike his efforts failed to earn much money, though today his works fetch high prices. The family spent their holidays every year in Sligo, which Susan and the children much preferred to London, and lived there for two entire years from 1872 to 1874.

7

8

7. Jack Butler Yeats, the poet's younger brother.

8. Susan Mary Yeats and Elizabeth Corbet Yeats, known as Lily and Lollie respectively, the poet's younger sisters.

9. William Butler Yeats as a child and a young man, 1865-94.
   a. with his nurse in Sligo, aged 7 months.
   b. with his uncle Fred Pollexfen in Sligo in 1872, aged 7.
   c. aged about 10.
   d. before 1889.
   e. about 1889.
   f-i. mid-1890s.

9

a

b

c

d

e

f

g

h

i

2. First Love and Early Mentors

In 1881 John Butler Yeats was in considerable financial difficulties and decided to move back to Dublin. He rented a studio in York Street, off St. Stephen's Green in Dublin city and settled his family near the sea at Howth, the large headland on the north east of Dublin Bay, where they spent two happy years. William became infatuated with his distant cousin LAURA ARMSTRONG (10) whom he saw one day driving a dog-cart round Howth, her red hair flying in the wind. He wrote a play for her called *Vivien and Time* and they corresponded, addressing each other as 'Clarin' and 'Vivien'. However, she was already engaged and got married on 17 September 1884.

William enrolled at the Erasmus Smith High School in Harcourt Street and accompanied his father each morning on the train to the city. Among his fellow pupils were W.K. MAGEE (12) who wrote under the name JOHN EGLINTON, and became an Assistant Librarian at the National Library of Ireland.

One of the first to encourage the young Yeats to write was THOMAS WILLIAM LYSTER (13), in later years Librarian of the National Library. In 1884 he helped Yeats to revise his dramatic poem *The Island of Statues,* taught him to correct proof sheets and guided his reading in Elizabethan literature.

Although a poor provider for his family in the financial sense, John Butler Yeats was a brilliant conversationalist and had many friends, among them EDWARD DOWDEN (11), who held the Chair of English Literature at Trinity College and was a noted poet and critic. He often stopped for breakfast in the York Street studio and listened to Yeats reciting his poems. After the Yeats family, again forced by financial exigencies, left Howth to live in Harold's Cross, Yeats visited Dowden's house in Rathgar where he met other young writers. However, Dowden proved to be out of sympathy with the Irish literary movement and Yeats attacked him in 1885 in his essay on Sir Samuel Ferguson.

10. Laura Armstrong, Yeats's first love.

11. Edward Dowden, Professor of English Literature at Trinity College, Dublin.

12. W.K. Magee, pseudonym 'John Eglinton', whom Yeats first met at school.

13. T.W. Lyster, Librarian of the National Library of Ireland, Yeats's early mentor.

10

11

12

13

3. The Contemporary Club

In 1885 Yeats attended informal Saturday night meetings in the rooms of CHARLES HUBERT OLDHAM (17) in Trinity College. Among the topics discussed was the editorial policy of the shortlived *Dublin University Review* which first published Yeats's work. Oldham was a Protestant Home Ruler and the College authorities, fearing that his meetings had too radical a tone, soon insisted that he hold them outside the College walls. So the Contemporary Club was founded as a forum for discussion of matters political, literary and philosophical. Meetings were held every Saturday night at 116 Grafton Street, above Ponsonby's bookshop. Through the Contemporary Club both John and William Butler Yeats got to know most of intellectual Dublin. John Butler Yeats did not speak very often but made many drawings of members (17-19). William used the Club as a training ground in public speaking and debate. His bitterest opponent was JOHN F. TAYLOR (19), a Catholic barrister whose rhetorical skills often defeated Yeats. The membership included STEPHEN GWYNN (18), the journalist and M.P., T.W. ROLLESTON (16), editor of the *Dublin University Review,* later to play an important part in the Irish Literary Society and The Rhymers Club, DR. DOUGLAS HYDE (15), Gaelic scholar and folklorist, founder of the Gaelic League and first President of the Irish Republic, and DR. GEORGE SIGERSON (14), a medical man with literary interests who attended Maud Gonne in the eighteen nineties.

14. Dr. George Sigerson, Contemporary Club member.

15. Dr. Douglas Hyde (1860-1949), Gaelic scholar and Contemporary Club member.

16. T.W. Rolleston, Contemporary Club member.

17. Charles Hubert Oldham, Protestant Home Ruler, economist and founder of the Contemporary Club, sketched by John Butler Yeats.

18. Stephen Gwynn, sketched by John Butler Yeats at the Contemporary Club.

19. John F. Taylor, a Catholic barrister, Yeats's most dreaded opponent in debate, sketched by John Butler Yeats at the Contemporary Club.

14

15

16

7

8

19

4. John O'Leary

The most important member of the Contemporary Club and certainly the most influential as far as Yeats was concerned was JOHN O'LEARY (21), the Fenian who was editor of the Irish Republican newspaper *Irish People* from 1863 to 1865. In 1865 he was convicted on a charge of treason-felony and sentenced to twenty years penal servitude. Having served five years he was released on condition that he remain in exile for the remainder of his term. He returned to Dublin in January 1885 to live with his sister Ellen. He soon recognized Yeats's genius and encouraged him in the study of Irish history and literature and the use of Irish literary themes. Yeats regarded O'Leary almost as a father figure and later wrote '... from O'Leary's conversation, and from the Irish books he lent or gave me has come all I have set my hand to since'.

O'Leary used his contacts to get Yeats's work accepted by the *Gael,* the penny weekly of the Gaelic Athletic Association, and by the Irish-American newspapers the *Boston Pilot* and the *Providence Sunday Globe.* After the Yeats family moved again to London in 1887 O'Leary organized the subscriptions for Yeats's first collection of poems, *The Wanderings of Oisin* (20). Throughout the eighteen nineties O'Leary remained in close contact with Yeats, helping him with occasional small loans and encouraging him in his Irish literary activities. Yeats often stayed with him when in Dublin at his house in Clontarf.

20. An 1886 draft of *The Wanderings of Oisin* (1889).

21. John O'Leary (1830-1907), Irish revolutionary who encouraged Yeats to use Irish themes.

20

Oison and the Islands of youth

Patrick
Oison tell me the famous story
Why thou out liveth old and hoary
The bad old days thou were't men sing
Trapped of an amerous demon thing

5. Katharine Tynan

In June 1885 Charles Hubert Oldham brought William Butler Yeats out to Clondalkin on the outskirts of Dublin to visit KATHARINE TYNAN (22) at her father's house WHITEHALL (24). Andrew Tynan was a prosperous dairy farmer and a staunch Parnellite. The household was large and very hospitable. Yeats and his sister Lily became frequent visitors, sometimes returning with other visitors to Dublin on the early morning milkcart if the weather had been too bad to walk back the night before. It was his first close social contact with a Catholic family, and at first the practice of Sunday dancing slightly shocked him.

Katharine Tynan was already an established poet, having published a successful book of verse entitled *Louise de la Vallière*. She too came under O'Leary's influence and she and Yeats encouraged each other to use Irish themes. Years later she described the Yeats she saw at that time as having 'all the dreams and gentleness and generosity, without a trace of bitterness'.

Her poems were published in the *Irish Monthly* the editor of which was FR. MATTHEW RUSSELL, S.J. (23), brother of Lord Russell of Killowen. Soon he began to publish Yeats's poems as well.

Someone suggested to Yeats that Katharine Tynan was the kind of woman who might break her heart over a man, so he thought about proposing to her and may actually have done so. If he did he was rejected, and she later married Henry Hinkson. She and Yeats maintained a lifelong correspondence and friendship. They met for the last time in the late nineteen twenties, a few years before her death in 1931.

22. Katharine Tynan (1861-1931), poet and novelist, whom Yeats met first in 1885.

23. Father Matthew Russell, S.J., editor of *The Irish Monthly*, who published some of Yeats's early poems.

24. Whitehall in Clondalkin, home of Katharine Tynan, where Yeats and his sister used to visit.

22

23

24

6. Maud Gonne

'The troubling of my life began', Yeats later wrote, when MAUD GONNE (25a-g) arrived at the Yeats's house in London in January 1889 with a letter of introduction from Ellen O'Leary. Yeats was immediately smitten by her beauty, her stature — she was nearly six feet tall — and the power of her personality.

At that time she was twenty three and he was only a few months older. Her father was an English Colonel. She had been brought up mainly in Ireland and had acted as her father's hostess in Dublin where she achieved some success as a Society beauty. After her father's death in 1886 she went to Paris where she began a liaison with a French Boulangist politician, Lucien Millevoye, which lasted until 1900. They had two children but only one, a girl, survived. Millevoye was virulently anti-British and under his influence and because of her experience of evictions in Ireland Maud Gonne decided to devote herself to the Irish nationalist cause and to become the Irish Joan of Arc.

After their first meeting Yeats dined with her nearly every evening until she returned to Paris. They met at irregular intervals over the next decade. He involved her with his occult and theatrical enterprises and she involved him with her political activities. He was in love with her and frequently asked her to marry him. She maintained a distance and finally, in December 1898, told him of her relationship with Millevoye. She broke with Millevoye in 1900, but then met John MacBride whom she married in 1903. Yeats was devastated at the news.

25 (a-g). Maud Gonne (1866-1953), famous beauty and love of Yeats's life.

25

a

b

c

d

e

f

g

19

7. Irish Literary Societies

While living in London Yeats attended meetings of the Southwark Irish Literary Club founded by FRANCIS A. FAHY (26), a Galwayman and poet. Encouraged by John O'Leary and with the help of D.J. O'DONOGHUE (28) and T.W. Rolleston (16), the Southwark Club was transformed into the IRISH LITERARY SOCIETY, LONDON (27), with GAVAN DUFFY (29) as its President. Its opening lecture was postponed until 18 March 1893 in order to allow a sister society, The National Literary Society, to be set up in Dublin. Yeats was appointed Secretary of the National Literary Society's Libraries Sub-Committee with the job of establishing and supplying circulating libraries to country branches. This plan never got off the ground despite the enthusiastic efforts of both Yeats and Maud Gonne.

Yeats and Gavan Duffy both had schemes for a projected series of Irish books. Duffy wanted to publish scholarly and didactic works while Yeats envisaged a series of works of popular imaginative literature. Yeats opened negotiations with his publisher Fisher Unwin, but was dismayed to find on his return from a visit to Ireland that his erstwhile friend Rolleston had told Duffy of these negotiations and that Duffy had converted Fisher Unwin to his ideas. Yeats felt betrayed by Rolleston and much acrimonious debate followed in the London and Dublin Societies. The first volume issued by the NEW IRISH LIBRARY was Thomas Davis's *The Patriot Parliament of 1689* (30), an arid work which confirmed Yeats's fears and precluded the series from achieving any great popular success.

26. Francis A. Fahy, founder of the Southwark Irish Literary Club.

27. Officers and committee of the Irish Literary Society, London, which Yeats helped to found.

28. D.J. O'Donoghue, author of *Poets of Ireland*.

29. The Hon. Sir Charles Gavan Duffy (1816-1903), Irish nationalist and Australian statesman, who hijacked Yeats's negotiations for the 'New Irish Library'.

30. Title page of the first volume of the 'New Irish Library', a choice which Yeats did not approve.

IRISH LITERARY SOCIETY, LONDON.

—·*·*·*·*·*·*·*·—

OFFICERS :

President :
SIR CHAS. GAVAN DUFFY, K.C.M.G.

Hon. Secretary :
ALFRED PERCEVAL GRAVES, M.A.

Hon. Treasurer :
DANIEL MESCAL.

Committee :

R. BARRY O'BRIEN, *Chairman.* W. M. CROOK, B.A. *Vice-Chairman.*

REV. STOPFORD BROOKE, M.A.	MISS O'CONOR-ECCLES.
F. A. FAHY.	D. J. O'DONOGHUE.
T. J. FLANNERY.	J. G. O'KEEFFE.
MISS ELEANOR HULL.	EDWARD O'SHAUGHNESSY.
LIONEL JOHNSON.	DR. MARK RYAN.
M. MACDONAGH.	DR. JOHN TODHUNTER.

W. B. YEATS.

THE

PATRIOT PARLIAMENT

OF 1689

WITH ITS STATUTES VOTES AND PROCEEDINGS

THE NEW IRISH LIBRARY.

EDITED BY

Sir CHARLES GAVAN DUFFY, K.C.M.G.

ASSISTANT EDITORS:

DOUGLAS HYDE, LL.D., | T. W. ROLLESTON,
National Literary Society, | Irish Literary Society,
4 College Green, | Bloomsbury Mansion, Hart St.,
DUBLIN. | LONDON.

BY

THOMAS DAVIS

EDITED WITH AN INTRODUCTION

BY

THE HON. SIR CHARLES GAVAN DUFFY, K.C.M.G.

London
T FISHER UNWIN
PATERNOSTER SQUARE

Dublin **New York**
SEALY, BRYERS & WALKER | P. J. KENEDY
MIDDLE ABBEY STREET | BARCLAY STREET

MDCCCXCIII

8. Republican Activities

When Yeats was appointed to the Senate of the newly formed Irish Free State in 1922 he was told that he owed his elevation not so much to his literary eminence as to his involvement with the Irish Republican Brotherhood in the eighteen nineties. So far as is known, he never took the IRB oath, but always regarded himself as having been enrolled by John O'Leary.

During the eighteen nineties he spoke at commemorations of Irish patriots such as Robert Emmet, Thomas Davis and Parnell. In 1896 in London, T.W. Rolleston (16) invited him to join a splinter group of the IRB called the Irish National Alliance led by DR. MARK RYAN (31), which had connections with Irish-American societies. In 1897 Maud Gonne asked him to help her raise funds for a monument to Wolfe Tone in Dublin as part of the centenary celebrations of the 1798 Rising. Yeats was elected President of the Centenary Association for Great Britain and France, with Dr. Mark Ryan as Treasurer. At a convention in Dublin of delegates from the '98 Centenary Committees on the day of the official celebration of Queen Victoria's Jubilee, 22 June 1897, Yeats made an anti-British speech (32). That night there was rioting in Dublin and it was only with difficulty that he restrained Maud Gonne from taking part. He accompanied her on a fund-raising tour of England and Scotland, and the next year took his place in the procession and on the platform at the laying of the foundation stone of the Wolfe Tone monument (33).

FRANK HUGH O'DONNELL (34), to whom Yeats referred as 'the Mad Rogue' was Yeats's enemy in Republican circles. He betrayed a plot of Maud Gonne and purloined money intended for revolutionary activity for which he was threatened with death. Both Maud Gonne and Yeats pleaded that he should not be killed, and partly as a result of this incident, Yeats withdrew from political and revolutionary involvement.

31. Dr. Mark Ryan, leader of the Irish National Alliance, a splinter group of the Irish Republican Brotherhood.

32. Report in *The Freeman's Journal* of a speech made by Yeats on the day of Queen Victoria's Jubilee, 22 June 1897.

33. *The Freeman's Journal,* 16 August 1898.

34. Frank Hugh O'Donnell, to whom Yeats referred as 'the Mad Rogue'.

31

33

THE
WOLFE TONE COMMEMORATION.

YESTERDAY'S MAGNIFICENT DISPLAY IN DUBLIN.

THE GREAT PROCESSION,

IN WHICH THE DUBLIN TRADES AND THE BELFAST
ORGANISATIONS SHOW GRANDLY.

THE IRISH MUNICIPALITIES REPRESENTED IN STATE.

THE WHOLE COUNTRY SUPPLIES DELEGATES AND
CONTINGENTS.

THE ROUTE FROM RUTLAND-SQUARE TO STEPHEN'S
GREEN.

SCORES OF THOUSANDS IN THE STREETS.

INCIDENTS BY THE WAY.

HISTORIC SPOTS CONNECTED WITH WOLFE TONE.

THE CEREMONY OF LAYING THE FOUNDATION STONE OF THE MONUMENT.

A THRILLING SCENE.

ENTHUSIASM OF THE PEOPLE.

ADDRESSES BY MR. JOHN O'LEARY, MR. JOHN DILLON
MR. J. REDMOND, M.P.,
AND THE FOREIGN DELEGATES.

A RECORD DEMONSTRATION.

CARRIED OUT WITH COMPLETE SUCCESS.

32   Mr W B Yeates next proposed—"That this Convention of Irishmen assembled this 22nd day of June, 1897, declares its belief in the right of Ireland to freedom." (Applause). He said that as he went about the streets of Dublin at the present time it seemed to him that that resolution was necessary. He should not have thought that they would have had in Ireland after her history quite so obvious or quite so energetic a manifestation of the necessity of this resolution. The Irish people next year would be celebrating a jubilee of their own (applause). One wondered why their friends outside—he would not give them so much importance as to call them their enemies—were engaged in celebrating the present Jubilee. Was it because more than four millions of the Irish people had been forced to emigrate, or was it that a million of the people had died of starvation, or was it that Ireland had for many years been robbed of nearly three millions a year. His opinion was that this bunting was hung out from sheer snobbery (applause). It was done for the same reason that people sometimes sought to acquire English accents (hear, hear). He did not, however, think that they need trouble much about these people. This Jubilee celebration meant that England had grown rich upon the robbery of the world, because they had built up their empire by rapine and fraud (applause). Next year Irishmen would celebrate the centenary of '98 in a very different manner. They would be celebrating a holy and sacred cause, and let them all hope that from that celebration would arise a movement that would unite the Irish people once again (applause). All he had to say was if they could not agree to worship their own martyrs then they were a defeated and discredited people (renewed applause).

34

9. Hermeticists, Theosophists, and the Golden Dawn

Around 1884 or 1885 Yeats read A.P. Sinnett's *Esoteric Buddhism,* which had a profound effect on him. His fellow pupil at the Erasmus Smith High School, CHARLES JOHNSTON (35), also read it and as a result founded the Dublin Hermetic Society to investigate occult matters. He invited MOHINI MOHUN CHATTERJI (36), an Indian Theosophist, to Dublin in late 1885. Chatterji's exposition of Hindu doctrine made a lasting impression on Yeats who, over forty years later, rephrased some words of Chatterji's in his poem 'Mohini Chatterji'. Johnston went to see MADAME BLAVATSKY (37), head of the Theosophical Society in London, and the Dublin Hermetic Society became the Dublin Lodge of the Theosophical Society. Subsequently Johnston ran away with Madam Blavatsky's niece VERA (35) whom he married in Russia.

Yeats met GEORGE RUSSELL (38), at the Metropolitan School of Art in 1886. Russell was a visionary and a poet who wrote under the pseudonym Æ. In 1891 he moved in with a community of theosophists at 3 Upper Ely Place in Dublin. Yeats occasionally stayed there and in 1892 he and Russell painted murals on the walls of the front room of the house (see back cover). The artistic influence of William Blake, whose works Yeats was editing at this time, is evident.

While living in London Yeats frequented the house of Madame Blavatsky. In 1888 she founded the Esoteric Circle of the Theosophical Society. Yeats was one of its most active members and became Secretary of a Research Committee set up to carry out experiments in occult practices. His experiments went further than was intended and in 1890 was asked to resign from the Society.

This did not matter too much to him as he had already been initiated into the Order of the Golden Dawn by one of its chiefs, SAMUEL LIDDELL MACGREGOR MATHERS (39), who married MOINA BERGSON (40), sister of the philosopher Henri Bergson.

35. Charles Johnston, his wife Vera, his mother and his brother Lewis.

36. Mohini Mohun Chatterji, an Indian Theosophist who greatly impressed Yeats when he visited Dublin in 1885.

37. Madame Helena Petrovna Blavatsky (1831-91), a Russian who founded the Theosophical Society.

38. George Russell (1867-1935), pseudonym Æ, a visionary and poet whom Yeats met at the Metropolitan School of Art in 1886.

39. Samuel Liddell MacGregor Mathers, a chief of the Order of the Golden Dawn.

40. Moina Mathers, sister of Henri Bergson and wife of MacGregor Mathers.

35

36

37

38

39

40

The Golden Dawn was a society dedicated to the study of Rosicrucianism and ritual magic. ANNIE E.F. HORNIMAN (43), a friend of Moina from the Slade School of Fine Art helped to fund Mathers who moved to Paris in 1892 and left the running of the London Temple to the actress FLORENCE FARR (45). Other members included WILLIAM SHARP (44), who wrote mystic celtic tales and romances under the pseudonym 'Fiona Macleod', ALAN BENNETT (47), who later became a Buddhist monk, Yeats's uncle GEORGE POLLEXFEN (48) of Sligo and W.T. Horton whose cartoon of Yeats (46) illustrates many of Yeats's preoccupations during the eighteen nineties. Maud Gonne was a member for a short time until she decided the Order was too close to Freemasonry. For much of the nineties Yeats worked with her and Annie Horniman on a projected Irish mystical order to be based in the CASTLE OF HEROES (41) on Lough Key, Co. Roscommon.

A dispute arose between the members of the London Order and Mathers who had became increasingly dictatorial and odd. Mathers sent ALEISTER CROWLEY (42), the diabolist, to seize the London headquarters but Yeats evicted him and guarded the rooms against him. The members expelled Mathers, but trouble continued as Annie Horniman accused Florence Farr of laxity in her administration of the Order. Yeats was Annie Horniman's sole supporter, and they prepared comprehensive memoranda to prove their case, but were outvoted.

The Order continued to be plagued with dissent and scandal, but Yeats remained a member of it and its offshoot, the Stella Matutina, until about 1921. It probably disintegrated in 1923.

41. 'Castle of heroes', Lough Key, Boyle, Co. Roscommon, where Yeats hoped to establish a Celtic mystical order.

42. Aleister Crowley, diabolist, whom Yeats forcibly evicted from the London rooms of the Golden Dawn.

43. Annie Elizabeth Fredericka Horniman, friend of Moina Mathers and member of the Golden Dawn.

44. William Sharp who wrote as 'Fiona Macleod'.

45. Florence Farr, actress and Administratrix of the Golden Dawn in London.

46. Drawing of Yeats by W.T. Horton, a fellow member of the Golden Dawn, illustrating Yeats's interests during the eighteen nineties.

47. Alan Bennett who became a Buddhist monk.

48. George Pollexfen, Yeats's uncle, whom he introduced to the Golden Dawn.

41

42

43

44

45

46

47

48

27

10. London Friends

In 1887 John Butler Yeats moved his family back to London. They took a house at 3 BLENHEIM ROAD, BEDFORD PARK (53), close to the house of WILLIAM MORRIS (49), the poet and socialist, where Yeats met such notables as Prince Kropotkin, the Russian revolutionary, Sidney Crane Cockerell, and GEORGE BERNARD SHAW (52). He also frequented the house of WILLIAM ERNEST HENLEY (50), poet and editor of the *National Observer* and of the *New Review,* who published some of his poems. He met OSCAR WILDE (51) there, and spent Christmas Day of 1888 with the Wildes in Tite Street where Wilde read to him his essay 'The Decay of Lying'. In 1895, between Wilde's two trials, Yeats came to his house to give him letters of support he had collected from Irish men of letters, but Wilde was staying elsewhere.

Yeats's closest friend in London in the early eighteen nineties was LIONEL JOHNSON (54), whom he met after the publication of *The Wanderings of Oisin.* Johnson impressed Yeats with his elegance and erudition, and introduced him to the theories of Walter Pater. In 1895 Yeats was shocked to discover that Johnson was drinking heavily and the friendship cooled. Johnson died in 1902 as a result of a fall from a bar stool.

ARTHUR SYMONS (55) took Johnson's place as Yeats's closest friend. He was an authority on French Symbolism, and editor of *The Savoy* in 1896. Yeats found him very easy to talk to, and in 1895 left the family home to share rooms with him in Fountain Court, The Temple. Part of his reason for leaving home was that he wished to conduct an affair with OLIVIA SHAKESPEAR (56 a-b), a cousin of Lionel Johnson. She was a novelist, and treated Yeats with much sympathetic understanding. They lived together at 18

49. William Morris (1834-96), poet and socialist, whose house Yeats used to visit.

50. William Ernest Henley (1849-1903), poet and editor of the *National Observer,* said to have been the inspiration for R.L. Stevenson's pirate 'Long John Silver'.

51. Oscar Wilde (1854-1900), wit and dramatist who told Yeats 'I think a man should invent his own myth'.

52. George Bernard Shaw (1856-1950), socialist and dramatist whom Yeats met at Morris's house.

53. 3, Blenheim Road, Bedford Park, where the Yeats family lived from March 1888.

54. Lionel Pigot Johnson (1867-1902), poet and close friend of Yeats until his decline into alcoholism.

55. Arthur Symons (1865-1945), poet and critic with whom Yeats shared rooms in 1895.

49

50

51

2

53

54

55

Woburn Buildings for nearly a year until Yeats met Maud Gonne again and Olivia Shakespear realised that his affections lay irrevocably elsewhere. However, they remained friends and corresponded until her death in 1938.

Yeats, along with ERNEST RHYS (59), founded the Rhymers Club in early 1890 in order to meet the poets of his time. Members met weekly, usually in the Cheshire Cheese, a pub off Fleet Street. There was a strong Celtic flavour to the membership which included apart from Yeats himself and Rhys who was Welsh, T.W. Rolleston, JOHN TODHUNTER (57), adoptive Irishman Lionel Johnson, and others including ERNEST DOWSON (58), Arthur Symons, Richard Le Gallienne, and John Davidson (60). George Moore and Oscar Wilde were occasional guests. They published two anthologies of their work, *The Book of the Rhymers Club* and *The Second Book of the Rhymers Club*. Contrary to the myth later promulgated by Yeats, they did not all die young. Most of them lived to a prosperous old age.

56. a-b. Olivia Shakespear, a cousin of Lionel Johnson, with whom Yeats had an affair in the eighteen nineties.

57. John Todhunter (1839-1916), an Irish writer, one of the founder members of the Rhymers Club.

58. Ernest Dowson, poet and member of the Rhymers Club, author of the well known line 'They are not long, the days of wine and roses'.

59. Ernest Rhys, poet, member of the Rhymers Club, and editor of the 'Everyman's Library'.

60. 'Some persons of the 90s', a cartoon drawn by Sir Max Beerbohm in 1925. From left to right: Richard Le Gallienne, W.R. Sickert, Arthur Symons, George Moore, John Davidson, A. Harlacos, Charles Conder, Oscar Wilde, Sir William Rothenstein, Sir Max Beerbohm, Yeats, Aubrey Beardsley.

56

a

b

57

58

59

60

11. Lady Gregory and Coole

Yeats met LADY GREGORY (61) at Edward Martyn's house Tullira Castle, Co. Galway in the summer of 1896 when he was thirty one and she was forty four. The following summer he spent two months at her house COOLE PARK (62), the first of many summers he spent there. They collected folklore together and collaborated on theatrical enterprises. Lady Gregory looked after his health and provided ideal conditions for him to write. Coole Park became almost his home where he 'found at last what I had been seeking always, a life of order and labour, where all outward things were the image of an inward life'.

61. Lady Isabella Augusta Gregory (1852-1932), author of over forty plays, and Yeats's friend and benefactor.

62. Coole Park, home of Lady Gregory, where Yeats spent many summers.

63. Yeats, Lady Gregory and an unidentified man at Coole.

64 (a-i). Yeats from about 1902-1914.

61

62

63

a

b

c

d

e

f

g

h

i

12. The Dramatic Movement

Yeats had always been interested in poetic drama. At the age of eighteen he wrote a play 'Vivien and time' for Laura Armstrong, and when he met Maud Gonne in 1889 he promised to write *The Countess Cathleen* for her.

In 1890 he saw FLORENCE FARR (65, 67), acting in John Todhunter's *A Sicilian Idyll* in the Bedford Park Playhouse, and soon made her acquaintance. She was a close friend of George Bernard Shaw, was active in the Golden Dawn and worked with Yeats on his experiments in speaking verse to the psaltery (65) over the next decade. In 1894 she took the Avenue Theatre with the financial backing of Annie E.F. Horniman, also a member of the Golden Dawn, and there produced Yeats's play, *The Land of Heart's Desire* as a curtain raiser to Todhunter's *A Comedy of Sighs*.

GEORGE MOORE (70) the novelist and dramatist was in the audience and his friend EDWARD MARTYN

65. Florence Farr with her Dolmetsch psaltery which she used to accompany her speaking of verse.

66. Programme for the first production of *The Countess Cathleen* in 1899.

67. Florence Farr whom Yeats first saw in John Todhunter's *A Sicilian Idyll* in 1890.

68. Edward Martyn (1859-1923), dramatist, friend of George Moore and founder of the Irish Literary Theatre.

69. Lady Isabella Augusta Gregory, founder of the Irish Literary Theatre.

70. George Moore (1852-1923), novelist and founder of the Irish Literary Theatre.

65

❦ Irish Literary Theatre, ❦
1899.

✳

"THE COUNTESS CATHLEEN"
By W. B. YEATS,
AND

"THE HEATHER FIELD"
By EDWARD MARTYN,
Will be performed for the first time in

THE ANTIENT CONCERT ROOMS.

The Countess Cathleen, *May 8th, 12th, 13th, and Matinee May 10th.*

The Heather Field, *May 9th, 10th & Matinee May 13th*

BY A

Specially-selected Company of Professional Artistes
Under the General Management of

MISS FLORENCE FARR

STAGE MANAGER - - - MR BEN WEBSTER

MUSIC CONDUCTED BY HERR BAST & MR. P. DELANY.

Scenery and Hall arrangements by Mr. BRENDAN STEWERT.
Costumes by NATHAN, and CLARKSON, of London.

PRICES

Reserved & Numbered Seats, 4s.; Area, 2s. 6d.; Balcony, 1s.
Plan and Booking at Messrs. PIGOTT'S, Grafton St.

67

70

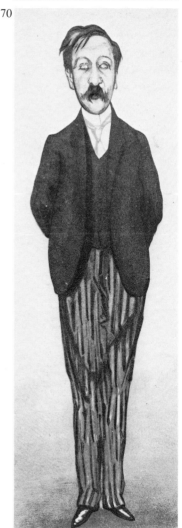

68

69

(68) introduced him to Yeats. Yeats visited Martyn at his home Tullira Castle, Co. Galway and there met LADY GREGORY (69). Yeats, Martyn, Lady Gregory and Florence Farr were soon discussing the possibility of establishing an Irish Literary Theatre to produce their plays. Their discussions resulted in the production of *The Countess Cathleen* and *The Heather Field* in the Antient Concert Rooms in Dublin in 1899 (66). George Moore was co-opted to help with the stage management and he and Yeats decided to collaborate further in the writing of a play based on the legend of Diarmuid and Grania, which they put on in 1901. However the Irish Literary Theatre's use of English actors who mispronounced Irish names gave rise to considerable criticism. This led Yeats and Lady Gregory, even before *Diarmuid and Grania* was produced, to associate themselves with the brothers Fay. FRANK FAY (72) was an accomplished speaker of verse and his younger brother WILLIAM (73) was a brilliant actor and stage manager. They had formed an 'Irish National Dramatic Group' and recruited their actresses from Maud Gonne's organisation Inghinidhe na hEireann (Daughters of Ireland). The first production they planned was George Russell's *Deirdre.* Yeats now offered them his *Cathleen Ni Houlihan* to accompany it. MAUD GONNE (71) played the title role in April 1902 and the play was a great success. The Irish National Theatre Society was then set up to be run on cooperative lines with Yeats as President, Maud Gonne, Douglas Hyde and George Russell as Vice-Presidents, and William G. Fay as stage manager. The Society put on several plays in 1903 and 1904, including Synge's controversial *In the Shadow of the Glen* and Yeats's *The Shadowy Waters* (72).

71. Scene from the 1902 production of *Cathleen Ni Houlihan,* with Maud Gonne in the title role.

72. Scene from the 1903 production of *The Shadowy Waters* in the Molesworth Hall with Maire Nic Shiubhlaigh (left) playing Dectora and Frank J. Fay taking the part of Forgael. The brass pin on Maire Nic Shiubhlaigh's head was a gift from Maud Gonne.

73. William G. Fay (1872-1947), actor and stage manager.

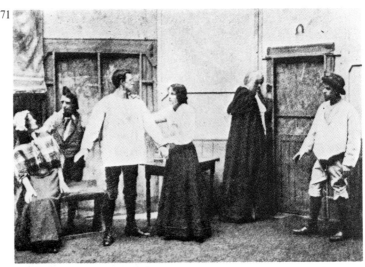

For some time past MISS HORNIMAN (74) had been watching the progress of the Society and talking about giving it financial backing. Now she made a definite commitment to provide £5,000, part of which would be used to convert the old Mechanics Institute on Abbey Street into a theatre, and part to provide an annual subsidy. Thus the Abbey Theatre opened on 27 December 1904 with plays by Lady Gregory, Yeats and Synge (76-78).

Despite initial success attendance soon dwindled. Yeats and Lady Gregory decided that a change in the cooperative structure of the Society was necessary. In 1905 they held a meeting of all the members which resulted in the transformation of the Society into a limited liability company. Yeats, Lady Gregory and J.M. SYNGE (75), were appointed Directors. The Fays and the actors were to be paid salaries. Some of the actors were unhappy with the changes and left.

In January 1907 the Abbey put on a new play by Synge, *The Playboy of the Western World*. To the audience of the time the play seemed 'an outrageous insult to the West of Ireland and its people' and riots ensued which were reported worldwide. On 4 February Yeats held a public meeting in the Abbey (79) where he defended the principle of free speech saying 'Every man has a right to hear (a play) and condemn it if he pleases, but no man has a right to interfere with another man hearing a play and judging for himself'. Two years later he ran up against the authorities of Dublin Castle on the same issue of free speech when they tried to prevent the staging of Shaw's *The Shewing Up of Blanco Posnet* which had been banned in England (80).

74. Annie E.F. Horniman, who provided the financial backing for the Abbey Theatre.

75. John Millington Synge (1871-1909), Director of the Abbey Theatre and author of its most controversial play *The Playboy of the Western World*.

76. Máire Nic Shiubhlaigh as Kathleen Ni Houlihan photographed from the auditorium on the opening night of the Abbey Theatre on 27 December 1904.

77. Poster for the opening of the Abbey Theatre.

78. Frank J. Fay as Cuchulainn in *On Baile's Strand* on the opening night of the Abbey Theatre.

79. Cartoon by Tom Lalor of Yeats addressing the audience from the stage of the Abbey on the occasion of the *Playboy* riots.

74

75

76

77

IRISH NATIONAL THEATRE SOCIETY

SPREADING THE NEWS
By LADY GREGORY.

ON BAILE'S STRAND
and

KATHLEEN NI HOULIHAN
By W. B. YEATS.

IN THE SHADOW OF THE GLEN
By J. M. SYNGE.

ABBEY THEATRE
TUESDAY. DEC. 27, '04
TO
TUESDAY, JAN. 3, '05.

Stalls, 2s.   Balcony, 2s.

78

79

AJAX YEATS DEFIES THE CENSOR.

Much excitement has been caused in Dublin owing to the determination on the part of the Abbey Theatre, of "Playboy of the West" notoriety, to produce a play of Bernard Shaw's in defiance of the warning of the Viceroy.

80. Cartoon published in the *Irish Weekly Independent,* 28 Aug. 1909, when Yeats and Lady Gregory insisted on staging Shaw's *The Shewing Up of Blanco Posnet* against the wishes of Dublin Castle.

81. Yeats continued to collaborate with the Abbey even though he was out of sympathy with its aims; his plight is satirized by his friend Edmund Dulac.

By this time the Fays had resigned, Synge had died from Hodgkin's disease, and conflict with Miss Horniman over theatre policy had led to her withdrawing her subsidy. The Abbey, with the help of English and American tours, was achieving some popular success as a 'people's theatre', but it was not the type of success that Yeats wanted. He had dreamed of creating an Irish heroic drama using ancient heroic symbols, new methods of speaking verse, and the kind of stage sets designed by Gordon Craig and Charles Ricketts. However, his poetic dramas never attracted large crowds as did Lady Gregory's and Synge's more realistic work. He began to withdraw more and more from active involvement with the Abbey. Ezra Pound, the young American poet, introduced him to the stylised Japanese Noh drama which provided him with a new dramatic form. He used it in *At the Hawk's Well* (82) first performed to a select audience in Lady Cunard's drawing room in London in 1916.

He maintained his links with the Abbey, always attended Board meetings when in Ireland, and was once again embroiled in controversy when he and Lady Gregory rejected Sean O'Casey's *The Silver Tassie* in 1928 (83). His last play *Purgatory,* was produced in the Abbey on 10 August 1938, a few months before his death.

82. (a-b). Designs by Gordon Craig for *At the Hawk's Well.*

83. Cartoon of Yeats rejecting Sean O'Casey's play *The Silver Tassie* in 1928.

84. Yeats pictured with a group from the Abbey Theatre circa 1930. Back row — Shelah Richards, Lennox Robinson, M.J. Dolan, F.J. McCormick, Denis O'Dea, Arthur Shields, Fred Johnson, P.J. Carolan. Front row — Maureen Delany, W.B. Yeats, May Craig, Eileen Crowe, unidentified, unidentified, Barry Fitzgerald.

82

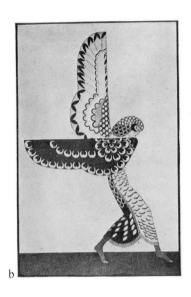

a

b

13. The Yeats Family in the U.S.A.

JOHN QUINN (88) was a wealthy lawyer, son of Irish immigrants to the United States. He had a passion for art and literature and first visited Ireland in 1902. There he met the Yeats family, Lady Gregory and most of the other leaders of the Irish Literary Revival. He arranged Yeats's first lecture tour of the United States at the end of the following year (85) and his later tours in 1911, 1914, and 1920. These tours enabled Yeats for the first time to earn substantial sums of money.

Yeats's sisters, Lily and Lollie were now working at DUN EMER, later Cuala Industries, Lily producing fine embroidery (86) and Lollie running a printing press (89). In 1906 Lollie went to New York for a few weeks to sell Dun Emer wares at the Irish Exhibition. The following year John Quinn suggested that Lily should visit after Christmas to attend another Irish Exhibition. At the last moment her father, JOHN BUTLER YEATS (87), now nearly seventy, decided to accompany her with the idea of gathering portrait commissions. He loved New York so much that he refused to come home, despite the entreaties of his family. He received some support from John Quinn, and from his son William, and died in New York in 1922 in his eighty third year.

85. Drawing of Yeats published in the New York newspaper, *The World,* 22 Nov. 1903.

86. The embroidery work room at Dun Emer, c. 1904. Lily Yeats is seated in front.

87. John Butler Yeats in 1907 at the time of his move to New York.

88. John Quinn (1870-1924), a wealthy New York lawyer, Yeats's patron and friend, with Yeats in 1914.

89. Lollie Yeats at the printing press in Dun Emer, c. 1904.

85

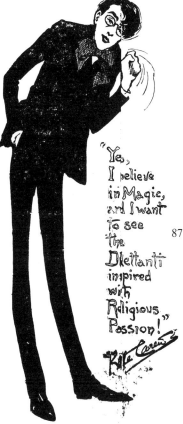

"Yes, I believe in Magic, and I want to see the Dilettanti inspired with Religious Passion!"

86

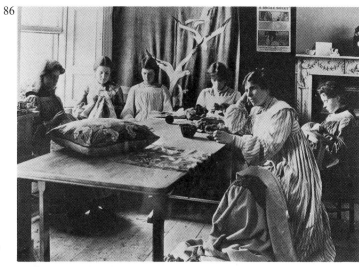

87

89

88

14. The Established Poet

During the first decade of this century most of Yeats's energy was absorbed by the theatre. So far as his personal life was concerned he was devastated by Maud Gonne's marriage to JOHN MACBRIDE (91) in 1903 and its subsequent break-up.

He still had his rooms in WOBURN BUILDINGS (92) and when in London entertained other poets including JOHN MASEFIELD (94) and ROBERT BRIDGES (93), both of whom became Poet Laureate.

His interest in the occult moved towards spiritualism. He attended a séance in London with COUNTESS MARKIEVICZ (90) sometime before her marriage, and went on to visit many mediums in England and America, and to experiment with automatic writing.

In 1910 he was awarded a Civil List pension, the following year he was appointed to the Academic Committee of the Royal Society of Literature, and in 1915 he was offered a knighthood which he refused.

He no longer wished to spend the winter in London, so in 1913 he moved to STONE COTTAGE (96) in Sussex with EZRA POUND (95), whom he had first met five

90. Countess Markievicz (1868-1927), with whom Yeats attended a séance in London.

91. John MacBride (1865-1916), a Boer War hero (on the Boer side), who married Maud Gonne.

92. Yeats in his study in Woburn Buildings in 1908.

93. Robert Bridges, Poet Laureate from 1913 and a visitor to Woburn Buildings.

94. John Masefield, Poet Laureate from 1930 and a visitor to Woburn Buildings.

95. Ezra Pound, poet and champion of the avant-garde.

96. Stone Cottage in Sussex which Yeats shared with Ezra Pound.

90

91

92

93

94

95

96

47

years earlier, and who had come to dominate his soirées in Woburn Buildings.

At the time of the outbreak of the first World War Yeats was in a state of depression. He began writing his memoirs, and in a poem published in *Responsibilities* asked his ancestors

'Pardon that for a barren passion's sake

Although I have come close on forty nine

I have no child, nothing but a book

Nothing but that to prove your blood and mine.'

In Ireland he was on the side of the Dublin workers in the 1913 Lockout. He supported Lady Gregory and HUGH LANE (98) in their struggle to establish a modern art gallery in Dublin, a struggle which prompted him to write 'September 1913' with its refrain

'Romantic Ireland's dead and gone,

It's with O'Leary in the grave.'

He was staying with Lord Rothenstein in England when the 1916 Easter Rising took place (99). He was first surprised and moved, and then shocked at the executions of the leaders of the Rising. He wrote 'Easter 1916' (97) a few weeks later. Among those executed was John MacBride, Maud Gonne's estranged husband. Yeats went to see her in Normandy, once again proposed to her and was once again refused.

While he stayed in Normandy ISEULT GONNE (100), Maud Gonne's daughter, acted as his secretary, and he now contemplated the possibility of marrying her. He had already, in 1912, met GEORGIE HYDE-LEES (101), the stepdaughter of Olivia Shakespear's brother by his first wife, and had seen her frequently since. In 1917 he returned to Normandy and repeated his proposal to Iseult which she refused. In September he proposed to Georgie Hyde-Lees, whom he called 'George'. She accepted, and they were married on 20 October 1917.

97. Manuscript draft of part of 'Easter 1916'.

98. Sir Hugh Lane (1875-1915), art dealer and collector who wished to establish a gallery of modern art in Dublin.

99. The Easter Rising of 1916 in Dublin.

100. Iseult Gonne from a pastel by her mother Maud Gonne.

101. Georgie Hyde-Lees whom Yeats married in 1917.

97
We know their dream; enough
To know they dreamed & died;
And what if excess of love
Bewildered them till they died?
I write it out in a verse—
MacDonagh & MacBride
And Connolly & Pearse
Now & in time to be
Wherever green is worn
Are changed, changed utterly;
A terrible beauty is born.

Sept 25. 1916

98

99

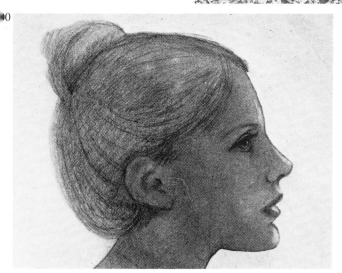

101

15. The Married Poet

The newly married couple went to Ashdown Forest for their honeymoon. A few days later George, to her husband's surprise, attempted automatic writing. What she wrote seemed to him so exciting and so profound that he offered to spend the remainder of his life 'explaining and piecing together those scattered sentences'. 'No' was the answer, 'we have come to give you metaphors for poetry.' In fact his wife's automatic writing formed the basis of *A Vision,* published first in 1926 and in a revised edition in 1937. This work is a 'system of symbolism', dealing with various types of human personality, with the 'gyres' of historical change, and with the supernatural. In the 1926 edition, not wishing to make known to the public his wife's automatic writing, he attributed the authorship of the major part of *A Vision* to GIRALDUS (103), a supposed sixteenth century philosopher.

Yeats had already bought THOOR BALLYLEE (105), a ruined Norman tower house in Gort, Co. Galway. He and his wife set about renovating it and spent part of every summer there until 1929. His first child, Anne Butler Yeats was born in 1919, and he set his poem 'A Prayer for my Daughter' (102) in Ballylee. A son, Michael, was born two years later.

In 1920 Yeats went on another lecture tour of the United States and introduced his wife to his father in New York. John Butler Yeats took to her at once, and as was his habit drew a sketch of her (106).

Meanwhile the War of Independence was raging in Ireland. The Yeatses spent much of the next two years in Oxford where Yeats denounced British policy in Ireland at the Oxford Union. He cultivated the company of the young and held Monday 'at homes' for undergraduates. Robert Bridges and John Masefield were both now resident in Oxford, and he enjoyed visits to Garsington, home of the literary hostess, LADY OTTOLINE MORRELL (104).

102. Manuscript draft of part of 'A Prayer for my Daughter'.

103. Yeats as Giraldus, the supposed author of part of *A Vision.*

104. Lady Ottoline Morrell, a literary hostess whose house Garsington Manor Yeats used to visit.

105. Thoor Ballylee, Gort, Co. Galway, the Yeatses' summer home.

106. Yeats's wife, sketched by his father while on a visit to New York in 1922.

102

Once more the storm is howling, & half hid
under this cradle hood & coverlid
~~My child sleeps on~~
my child ~~sleeping~~ sleeps on - There is obstacle
But Gregory's wood & one bare hill
where by the ~~~~ 's every wind
~~~~ can be checked,
~~~~ the storm ~~~~
But ~~~~ the storm ~~~~

104

105

106

51

16. The Sixty Year Old Smiling Public Man

In March 1922 Yeats moved from Oxford to 82 Merrion Square, Dublin. His old friend GEORGE RUSSELL lived one door up at No. 84 (107). The Civil War had begun. In August the bridge at Ballylee was blown up and in December bullets were fired into the Merrion Square house.

He was awarded an honorary degree by Trinity College, Dublin, and was appointed to the Senate of the newly formed Irish Free State (108). The following year he went to Stockholm to receive the Nobel prize (109). He remained in the Senate until 1928 and aroused controversy in 1925 with a speech in favour of divorce. He was Chairman of the Committee which chose the coinage of the new state, took an interest in education, and went on a tour of primary schools which led to his composing 'Among Schoolchildren' (110), in which he depicts himself as 'A sixty year old smiling public man'. He was friendly with Kevin O'Higgins and his wife and was deeply shocked when O'Higgins was assassinated.

107

107. Chin angles or how the poets passed. The story is told in Dublin that W.B. Yeats and George Russell (Æ) set out respectively from 82 and 84 Merrion Square to see each other ... and passed at 83. This drawing shows how it happened.

108. Yeats arriving at the Senate, from *Irish Life,* January 1923.

109. Yeats received the Nobel Prize in December 1923.

110. Manuscript draft of part of Yeats's poem 'Among schoolchildren'.

MR. YEATS IN STOCKHOLM.

RECEIVES NOBEL PRIZE.

PRESENTED BY THE KING OF SWEDEN.

—◆—

1

I walk through the long school-room questioning
A kind old nun in a white hood replies;
The children learn to cypher & to sing,
To study reading-books & histories,
To ~~different and~~ ~~eat~~
To ~~neatened~~ sow ₍neat₎ in every thing
In the best modern way — the childrens eyes
In momentary wonder stare upon
A sixty year old smiling, public-man.

In 1926 Yeats was a member of the memorial committee to his old friend T.W. Lyster, Librarian of the National Library of Ireland (111), and on 23 March 1926 made the speech on the occasion of the unveiling of the memorial outside the Library's Reading Room.

111. Some members of the T.W. Lyster memorial committee photographed on the steps of the National Library of Ireland in 1926. From left to right: E.H. Alton, Sir Philip Hanson, W.B. Yeats, R.L. Praeger, Richard I. Best, George Atkinson, L.C. Purser.

112 (a-i). Yeats from about 1922 to 1938.

111

112

a

b

c

d

e

f

g

h

i

Living in Merrion Square Yeats maintained his habit of having Monday evening 'at homes' for other and younger writers. Among those who frequented his house were F.R. HIGGINS (116) a young poet who later managed the Abbey Theatre and edited the Cuala Broadsides, LENNOX ROBINSON (116), a dramatist who had managed the Abbey for many years, Walter Starkie and FRANK O'CONNOR (113) who were also involved with the running of the Abbey, FRANCIS STUART (115), a novelist who married Iseult Gonne, LIAM O'FLAHERTY (114), another novelist, and Sean O'Faolain, a short story writer.

In 1932 Yeats, along with George Bernard Shaw, founded the Irish Academy of Letters with the aim of promoting creative literature in Ireland and overcoming obstacles to creative activity, including censorship. Yeats undertook an American tour in order to raise funds. The Academy instituted several awards, including the Harmsworth Prize which was presented to LORD DUNSANY (117) for his novel *The Curse of the Wise Woman* in 1934.

113. Frank O'Connor, i.e. Michael O'Donovan, short story writer.

114. Liam O'Flaherty, novelist.

115. Francis Stuart, novelist who married Iseult Gonne.

116. F.R. Higgins and Lennox Robinson, both managers of the Abbey Theatre. Higgins was a poet and edited the Cuala Broadsides.

117. Lord Dunsany, left, being presented with the Harmsworth Prize of the Irish Academy of Letters by F.R. Higgins (centre) and Yeats.

113

114
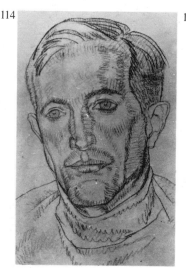

115

57

17. Last Years

In July 1932 Yeats and his family moved to Riversdale, a house in Rathfarnham outside Dublin. Among the visitors there was a Captain Dermot MacManus, a member of the Army Comrades Association which became known as the BLUESHIRTS (118). Yeats was attracted by Blueshirt ideas and invited the Blueshirt leader General O'Duffy to his house. He wrote three marching songs for the movement, but soon became disillusioned and rewrote the songs so that nobody could sing them.

During the nineteen thirties Yeats was troubled more and more by ill health and underwent several operations. He continued to interest himself in younger writers including DOROTHY WELLESLEY, wife of the Duke of Wellington (119), who edited some of the Cuala Broadsides, Ethel Mannin and MARGOT RUDDOCK (121), a young poet whose verse speaking ability he admired and used in radio broadcasts.

Ill health forced him to spend more time abroad, and he passed the winter of 1935 to 1936 in Majorca with SHRI PUROHIT SWAMI (120), an Indian monk whom he had known for some years, and with whom he collaborated on a translation of the Upanishads.

118. Blueshirts on parade.

119. Dorothy Wellesley, Duchess of Wellington, a poet whom Yeats admired.

120. Shri Purohit Swami, with whom Yeats worked on a translation of the Upanishads.

121. Margot Ruddock, a young poet encouraged by Yeats.

118

119

120

121

His idiosyncratic selection of poems for the 1936 edition of the *Oxford Book of Modern Verse* aroused considerable controversy. The following year he made a series of broadcasts for the BBC (122).

By this time many of his old friends including Florence Farr, John Quinn, Katharine Tynan, Lady Gregory, George Russell, Miss Horniman and Olivia Shakespear, were dead. Yeats himself, however, continued working, publishing *New Poems* in 1938. In November 1938 he left London with his wife for the South of France. On the following 28 January he died and was buried at Roquebrune. His *Last Poems and Two Plays* and *On the Boiler* were published posthumously.

In 1943 his body was reinterred in Drumcliffe Churchyard, Sligo (123).

122. Yeats broadcasting at the B.B.C. in 1937.

123. The grave of W.B. Yeats in the churchyard at Drumcliffe, Co. Sligo.

Cast a cold Eye
On Life, on Death.
Horseman, pass by!

W. B. YEATS

June   13th   1865
January   28th   1939

Acknowledgements

We wish to express our thanks to Anne and Michael Yeats for permission to reproduce photographs and manuscripts.

Despite strenuous efforts it has not been possible to locate the copyright holders of all the items reproduced. Thanks are due to Rex Roberts Studios, 2, 9a-b, 48, 86, 89, 101, 106; Professor John Kelly, St. John's College, Oxford, 10, 53, 56b; J. Fraser Cocks III, Special Collections Librarian, Colby College, Maine, U.S.A., 12; National Gallery of Ireland, 17, 81; Hugh Lane Municipal Gallery of Modern Art, 31; Trinity College Dublin, 36; Theosophical Society in Britain, 37; Radio Times Hulton Picture Library, 49, 50, 61, 64, 94, 104; Sir Rupert Hart-Davis and Ashmolean Museum, 60; Lionel Kelly, Dept. of English, Reading University, 64i; Professor William M. Murphy, Schenectady, New York, 88; Library of Congress, Washington, 87; Beinecke Rare Book Collection, Yale, 95, 96; Bord Fáilte, 105, 123; George Morrison, 118; BBC, 122.

The assistance of the following is gratefully acknowledged: Bill Bolger and Michael Walsh of the National College of Art and Design; Professor Brendan Kennelly who read the text; Dr. Goodwin MacDonnell and Isabel Gilsenan of 3 Ely Place; L. Storey, Theosophical Society in Britain; Mrs. Norah Tynan Wayte; Peter Tynan O'Mahony.

Special thanks are due to the staff of the National Library of Ireland, and especially to Dónall O Luanaigh, Keeper of Printed Books, Dr. Noel Kissane, Education Officer, Eugene Hogan, Photographer, Tom Desmond, Mairin Curran, Laura Dillon, and Brian McKenna and Gerard Lyne of the Department of Manuscripts. The assistance of John Farrell and of the Director of the National Museum of Ireland in mounting an associated exhibition, is also acknowledged.

Bibliographic Sources

Bachchan, Harbans Rai: W.B. Yeats and occultism. New York, Weiser, 1974.
Bax, Clifford: Some I knew well. London, Phoenix, 1951.
Cammell, Charles Richard: Aleister Crowley. London, Richards, 1951.
Colquhoun, Ithell: Sword of wisdom: MacGregor Mathers and 'The Golden dawn'. London, Spearman, 1975.
Denson, Alan: Printed writings by George W. Russell (AE): a bibliography. London, Northwestern U.P., 1961.
Ellmann, Richard: Eminent domain. New York, O.U.P., 1967.
Fay, W.G. and Catherine Caswell: The Fays of the Abbey Theatre. London, 1935.
Flannery, Mary Catherine: Yeats and magic. Gerrards Cross, Smythe, 1977.
Fraser, G.S.: W.B. Yeats. London, British Council, 1954.
Gordon, D.J.: W.B. Yeats: images of a poet. Manchester U.P., 1961.
Harper, George Mills: W.B. Yeats and W.T. Horton. London, Macmillan, 1980.
Harper, George Mills, ed.: Yeats and the occult. London, Macmillan, 1976.
Harper, George Mills: Yeats's Golden Dawn. London, Macmillan, 1974.

Hone, Joseph: W.B. Yeats 1865-1939. London, Macmillan, 1942.

Hunt, Hugh: The Abbey: Ireland's National Theatre 1904-78. Dublin, Gill and Macmillan, 1979.

Jeffares A. Norman and K.G.W. Cross, edd.: In excited Reverie. London, Macmillan 1965.

Jeffares, A. Norman: W.B. Yeats, man and poet. London, 2nd ed: Routledge and Kegan Paul, 1962.

Johnson, Lionel: Poetical works. London, Elkin Mathews, 1915.

Krans, Horatio Sheafe: William Butler Yeats and the Irish literary revival. New York, 1904.

Le Gallienne, Richard: The Romantic '90s. London, Putnam, 1951.

Levenson, Samuel: Maud Gonne. London, Cassell, 1977.

Longaher, Mark: Ernest Dowson, 3rd ed: Philadelphia, University of Pennsylvania Press, 1967.

Longenbach, James: Stone Cottage. New York, Oxford University Press, 1988.

Mac Liammóir, Mícheál and Eavan Boland: W.B. Yeats and his world. London, Thames and Hudson, 1971.

Malins, Edward: A Preface to Yeats. London, Longman, 1974.

Malins, Edward: Yeats and music. Dublin, Dolmen, 1968 (Dolmen Press Yeats Centenary Papers).

Malins, Edward: Yeats and the Easter Rising. Dublin, Dolmen, 1965 (Dolmen Press Yeats Centenary Papers).

Murphy, William M.: Prodigal father: the life of John Butler Yeats. Ithaca, Cornell University Press, 1978.

O'Donnell, F. Hugh: A History of the Irish Parliamentary Party. Vol. 1. London, Longman, 1910.

O'Driscoll, Robert and Lorna Reynolds, edd.: Yeats and the theatre. London, Macmillan, 1975.

Oshima, Shotaro: W.B. Yeats and Japan. Tokyo, Hokuseido Press, 1965.

Reid, Forrest: W.B. Yeats. London, Secker, 1915.

Rolleston, C.H.: Portrait of an Irishman: a biographical sketch of T.W. Rolleston. London, Methuen, 1939.

Russell, Matthew: The Life of Mother Mary Baptist Russell. New York, 1901.

Ryan, W.P.: The Irish literary revival. London, 1894.

Swami, Shri Purohit: An Indian monk. London, Macmillan, 1932.

Symons, Arthur: Studies in prose and verse. London, Dent, (1905).

Symons, Arthur: Studies in strange souls. London, 1929.

Todhunter, John: From the land of dreams. Dublin, Talbot Press, 1918.

Tuohy, Frank: Yeats. Dublin, Gill and Macmillan, 1976.

Unterecker, John, ed.: Yeats and Patrick McCartan: a Fenian friendship. Dublin, Dolmen, 1967 (Dolmen Press Yeats Centenary Papers).

Wade, Allan: A Bibliography of the writings of W.B. Yeats. London, Hart-Davis, 1951.

Yeats, W.B. and Margot Ruddock: Ah, sweet dancer: a correspondence. Edited by Roger McHugh. New York, Macmillan, 1970.

Yeats, W.B.: Autobiographies. London, Macmillan, 1955.

Yeats, W.B.: The collected letters of W.B. Yeats. Vol. 1: 1865-95. Edited by John Kelly and Eric Domville. Oxford, Clarendon, 1986.

Yeats, W.B.: The letters of W.B. Yeats. Ed. by Allan Wade. London, Hart-Davis, 1954.

Yeats, W.B.: Memoirs. Transcribed and edited by Denis Donoghue. London, Macmillan, 1972.